Getting to know Korea

GETTING TO KNOW KOREA

Written and Illustrated by REGINA TOR

With the world getting smaller and smaller, everyone should know as much as possible about how other people live. Boys and girls will wonder about these real people— the Koreans. What do they wear, what do they eat, do they have schools like ours and play games like we do? All these questions and many more are answered in this book with clever illustrations as well as maps.

* *

Getting to know

KOREA

Regina Tor

THIS SPECIAL EDITION IS PUBLISHED BY ARRANGEMENT WITH
THE PUBLISHERS OF THE REGULAR EDITION
COWARD—McCANN, INC.
BY

E. M. HALE AND COMPANY
EAU CLAIRE, WISCONSIN

TO

PEACE

IN OUR WORLD

KOREA

is a country which sticks, like a finger, straight out into the sea. In fact, it sticks straight out between two seas— the Yellow Sea and the Sea of Japan.

If you look closely at the map, you will see that Korea is right over there, on the other side of the Pacific Ocean, between China and Japan.

RICE BOWL

This country shaped like a finger has a nickname. It is called the Land of the Morning Calm, and it is a very beautiful land indeed.

It is neither very cold (like Alaska) nor very hot (like Africa).

It's just medium. Much the same as it is here in America. Snow flies in the winter and, in the springtime, flowers turn Korean hills blue, pink, and bright yellow.

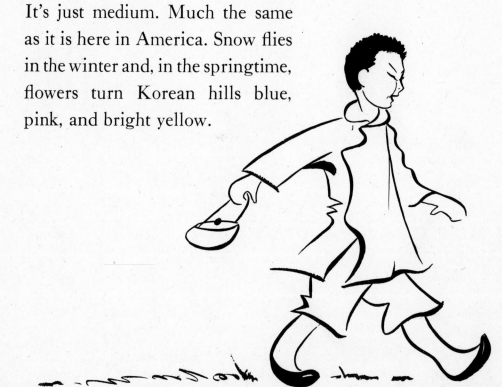

During July and August it rains almost every day. But then comes September and scarlet leaves and crisp, blue-sky days. School bells ring and children, swinging brass rice bowls in little string bags, hurry off to school.

Yes, except for the tip of the finger where hills are bare and rock-ribbed, Korea is a truly delightful land. In the south, wide valleys rise gently up to rolling green hills. Throughout much of the country there are tall forests, dark and cool and deeply shaded. And in the north, bold mountains hold swift streams and small villages.

These streams, clear and cool and bubbling
with laughter, spring from narrow cracks
in the mountains; jump, singing, down the
face of mountains. On their downward run,
they join with other streams, become wider,
deeper, less playful.

When they finally reach the valleys, they flatten them-
selves out into broad, grown-up rivers. Now they are
ready to work; ready to help the farmer water his crops,
and ready to carry the people to and from the cities and
towns.

Rivers are very important in Korea. They are the water-roads of the country. Hundreds of boats loaded with people, sacks of rice, and baskets of fruits and vegetables use them every day.

Many of the people in Korea live, like most of you, in towns. In the north, the people are miners or lumberjacks or workers in shoe and clothing factories. In the south, the people are farmers.

RICE PLANTING

Many of the crops these people grow are the same ones American farmers grow—rice, beans, peas, barley, cotton, and tobacco. Some, of course, are different. Castor beans for instance. From this bean comes castor oil, used now for greasing airplane engines.

TOQUES—
FOR STORING FOOD

Millet is another crop which isn't grown much here in America, but in Korea millet is very important. It is a grain which is eaten as a cereal. It is also used to make bread. And its tall strong stalks are made into mats, and fences, and even houses.

HOME OF A WEALTHY KOREAN

Most houses, however, are made of a mixture of stone and mud. This mixture, which is much like our concrete, makes a sturdy house indeed. Heavy posts of wood stand at the four corners of the house. These posts, which are often hand-carved and decorated, support the stone and mud walls. The roofs are made of tile or thatched with straw. Many of the houses are painted white, and sometimes their doors are painted red or blue.

If you were to walk into a Korean house, you would step first into a large central hall. Here, in the hall, you would see a fish head and a bunch of red peppers hanging from one of the beams in the ceiling.

This fish-head-and-peppers is more than a decoration. It means that the family who lives here prays that there will always be food for their people to eat.

You see, in south Korea there is often the danger of floods and dry-spells, both of which ruin crops. And when the crops are ruined, there is a great sadness in the land. The south Koreans (who are the farmers) and the north Koreans (who depend upon the farmers in the south for food) both go hungry and grow poor and sad.

It is to guard against such a sadness that Koreans hang a fish-head and a bunch of red peppers in their halls.

OXEN CARRY CROPS AS WELL AS PLOW FIELDS

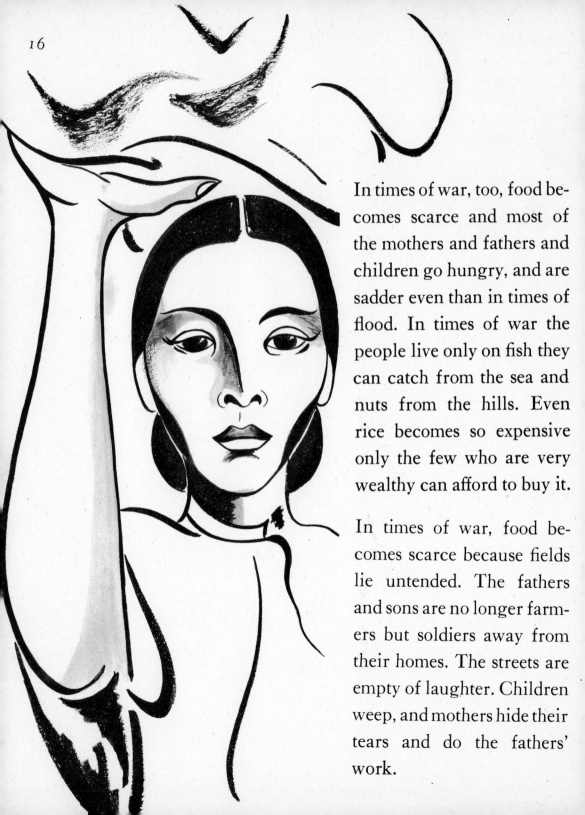

In times of war, too, food becomes scarce and most of the mothers and fathers and children go hungry, and are sadder even than in times of flood. In times of war the people live only on fish they can catch from the sea and nuts from the hills. Even rice becomes so expensive only the few who are very wealthy can afford to buy it.

In times of war, food becomes scarce because fields lie untended. The fathers and sons are no longer farmers but soldiers away from their homes. The streets are empty of laughter. Children weep, and mothers hide their tears and do the fathers' work.

The Korean people have suffered much. They know well the sadnesses of war, and the joy that comes only with peace.

In the good years, in the years of no wars and no floods and no droughts, you would find in Korea many of the same foods you find here in America: roast beef, pork, and chicken; fish, potatoes, green vegetables, and fresh fruits.

There are also other foods, such as octopus and eel, which we don't eat much here in America yet, but which are said to be delicious.

OCTOPUS

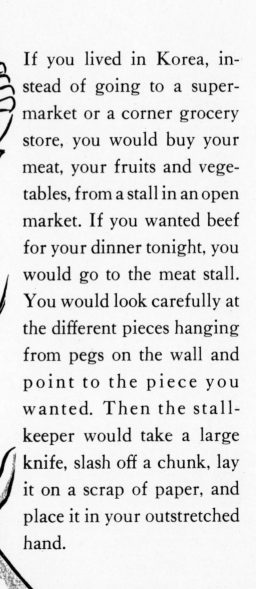

If you lived in Korea, instead of going to a supermarket or a corner grocery store, you would buy your meat, your fruits and vegetables, from a stall in an open market. If you wanted beef for your dinner tonight, you would go to the meat stall. You would look carefully at the different pieces hanging from pegs on the wall and point to the piece you wanted. Then the stall-keeper would take a large knife, slash off a chunk, lay it on a scrap of paper, and place it in your outstretched hand.

You would thank him, pay him, and
move on down the line, choosing vegetables from baskets and bowls, fruit from
a tray. You might spy a chicken, alive,
in a slatted cage; a chicken that looked
particularly plump and delicious. You
would point again, ask "How much?",
agree on a price, and carry it home for
tomorrow's lunch.

Mixed in with the meats, the vegetables and fruits and
sacks of rice, you would find flowers, scarves of silk, and
kites for sale.

Your mother might be surprised to find no frozen, no
canned foods in the market. In a few large cities (like
Seoul) she would find these things in bright modern
stores, but in most Korean towns she would have to shop,
as you just did, in the open air.

Your mother might be surprised too at the kitchen of a Korean house. This kitchen is dug down about two feet below the level of the earth—like a shallow cellar. Along one side of the room is a counter made of rocks and mud, with openings in the side for fires. Directly above these fires, plastered securely down into holes in the top of the counter, are big iron pots. This counter (like a long, low fireplace without a chimney) is a Korean mother's stove.

Her refrigerator is a collection of brown crocks called "toques," which she keeps outside. A few of these toques are buried beneath the ground before the first frost, preserving her special foods until spring.

MARU
WHERE FOOD IS PREPARED

Preparations for dinner in a Korean home start early in the afternoon, for there are many jobs to be done. Water must be hauled in from outside and fuel broken up for the fire. The mother washes the vegetables by dunking them up and down, first in one pan of water and then in another to make sure that they are really clean.

When everything is ready, the pots steaming hot, she puts her dinner on to cook over the smoking fire. She cooks the way you do when you go camping. You can easily understand that making dinner for a hungry Korean family takes a great deal of time. It is also very hard work.

A KOREAN STOVE

GATE TO SEOUL

SITTING ON THE TOP OF A HILL, SEOUL IS SURROUNDED BY A WALL AS TALL AS A 3-STOREY HOUSE, OLD AND CRUMBLING.

In Korea, the big cities, of course, are much like big cities anywhere, with many fine restaurants and hotels, modern theatres, and department stores, busy streets, noise, and bright lights at night.

In Seoul, which is the capital of Korea, there are more than two million people living, working and playing together. Sitting on the top of a hill, Seoul is surrounded by a very high, old wall. In some places this wall is more than twenty feet high.

Every day, through the huge gates in this wall, come hundreds of people from the country with their loads of rice, eggs, and chickens; their mats and their pottery jars. In the big market place they spread out their wares and squat before them, gossiping and smoking their long-stemmed clay pipes and trading their wares for those of their neighbors.

EGGS

ARE SOLD BY THE 'STICK'. EGGS ARE LAID END TO END AND WRAPPED TIGHTLY WITH STRAW.

A Korean market is not only a place in which to sell your food and utensils. It is also a place to meet friends, hear the latest news from the town up the river, and plan, maybe, for *Hwanggap*.

Hwanggap is a feast given for an old man, or his wife, when he reaches his sixtieth birthday. It is a very old Korean custom. Dressed in white and wearing his tall black hat, straight and proud, the old man sits outside his house.

In front of him, on a low table, are placed the various dishes of the feast; many many dishes of special holiday foods, enough to give even a young man a whole day of tasting and nibbling.

During this feast, the people of the town come to greet the old man. They sip rice wine together, wishing "Good Health," and then the old men in happiness get up and dance the old Korean folk-dances.

Hwanggap is a gay and happy holiday. It is a man's most important birthday. It is a day set aside in Korea to honor the "old man" of the family, the old man for whom everyone has the deepest respect.

When the feast is over, the women take the white clothes, soiled now from so much merrymaking, and wash them sparkling clean again.

Korean women wash their clothes by scrubbing them over rocks by the river banks, and then they spread them out in the sun to dry. When the clothes are dry, the women beat them with two sticks. Piece by piece, each jacket, shirt and pair of pants is beaten smooth again. This is hard work. It is a job Korean women dislike very much, for it takes a long time to iron clothes smooth by beating them with sticks.

IRONING IS A TIME FOR VISITING, FOR IT IS ALWAYS DONE IN PAIRS

A Korean woman is small compared to most American women. Her hair of shiny black is parted in the middle and tucked neatly up in the back. Her skin is the color of ivory. She has high cheek bones and almond-shaped eyes, and her cheeks are as red as a June-ripe cherry.

She stands as straight as a birch tree, for on her head she carries bundles of laundry, baskets of food, all kinds of things. She is dignified and quiet, not laughing much. But when she walks she looks as if she were skipping little skips down the street.

Most of the women wear wide, shirred skirts which reach the ankles. Over the skirt they wear a shirt of silk or cotton in a bright color. This shirt is almost exactly like the man's and is worn, as his is, on the outside rather than tucked in.

Around her waist, in a sling made from a shawl, a woman carries her baby.

On her tiny feet she wears thin rubber shoes. These shoes look like those rubbers your mother wears, the ones which cover only the soles of her high-heeled shoes.

A Korean woman wears various types of caps and hats— to shield her from the sun while she works in the fields, to protect her from the cold, or to dress-up for town. And sometimes, when she goes to a party, she ties a silk scarf over her perfumed hair.

The country men, for the most part, still dress in the native costume of white. A shirt of white is worn over white trousers which are very full, like pantaloons. The men fold these trousers around their waists, letting them hang loose at the hips, and then wrapping them tightly about their ankles.

Men over sixty-five wear black hats made of horsehair, with a narrow brim and a high crown. This hat looks a bit like a top hat made of wire window screen. It was designed for the topknot of hair which all men used to wear just as soon as they were married, and which some of the older ones still do wear.

THROWING CASH·PIECES

KOREAN CHILDREN HAVE FEW TOYS BUT MANY GAMES.

Young boys, a long time ago, wore their hair in a single braid down their backs. Today most boys wear their hair cut short like yours.

Many of the children, both boys and girls, wear the same kind of clothes Korean children have always worn; shirts and trousers in gay colors of blue, pink, and pale green. Of course, some of the children in Seoul, where there are big department stores selling American and European clothes, dress just as you and your class-mates do.

You would like these Korean children. Their eyes are black and shiny. So is their hair. They run and chatter, toss balls in the air, giggle and laugh. And some days, like you, they give their teachers a terrible time. But only some days. Most days they study very hard (like you).

In their schools they study, as you do, geography, history, science, and arithmetic. Instead of English, of course, they study their own language, Korean-Chinese.

THE NEW YEAR'S HOLIDAY
BRINGS A TRAVELING SIDE-
SHOW TO EVERY VILLAGE.
THE STAR ACTORS ARE A
MONKEY AND A TIGER.
NEW YEAR'S LASTS 15 DAYS.

In their schoolyards they play games of ball and hop-scotch. And on Saturdays they take their big brightly-colored kites up into the hills to fly with the winds from the sea.

Korean children spend a great many evenings with their fathers, who tell them stories of long ago when there were no radios or trains or buses in Korea. For traveling about, there were just ponies and jinrickshas and sedans.

Sedans are chairs, with roofs and no legs, fastened to two poles and carried about on the shoulders of men.

Jinrickshas are small hooded carriages with two big wheels and two long poles sticking out in front. One or more men stand between these two poles and pull the carriage along.

SWING DAY
MAY 30, IN EVERY VILLAGE, A CONTEST. PRIZE GOES TO THE COUPLE WHO SWINGS THE HIGHEST.

The name "jinricksha" is a combination of three Japanese words: jin (meaning "man"), riki ("power"), and sha ("carriage"). So, the name "jinricksha" means actually a man-powered carriage.

JINRICKSHA

BUDDHA WAS A RELIGIOUS TEACHER WHO LIVED IN ASIA A VERY LONG TIME AGO. BUDDHISM, CONFUCIANISM, AND CHRISTIANITY ARE PRACTICED IN KOREA AS WELL AS ANIMISM.

BUDDHA

The fathers tell their children, too, of the days long ago when Koreans were teaching the Japanese how to weave cloth, how to raise silkworms, and how to print books and paint pictures. Yes, this was a very long time ago when Koreans wore their money like beads on strings.

Listening to their fathers, Korean children learn that their country is a land of tall, beautiful forests; forests of pine, maple, birch, and oak; and that their country possesses a wealth of gold and silver and tungsten. Tungsten, as you all know, is very important for it is the metal from which the wire is made that lights up inside your electric bulb.

The children learn too that every year from the deep clear sea surrounding their country on three sides, come millions of tons of fish.

You would like the quaint fishing boats with their billowing sails. Blown by the winds of the sea, they move gracefully in and out between the islands off the west coast.

Along some parts of Korea's shore, steep cliffs rise straight up from the water's edge. In other parts, green hills slope gently back to the middle country.

Standing on the edge of the shore and looking straight down through the sparkling water, you can see great beds of rainbow-colored coral, delicate and fairy-like, through which strange fish dart and play.

At the great seaport of Pusan, big ships from China and Japan load up with lumber from Korea's forests, rice from her valleys, and fish from the sea. Then, with a great hooting and whistling, the big ships steam out of the harbor and head back toward home.

A seaport is a very exciting place.

"YUT-SA-SEE-OH"

"BUY YOUR YUT HERE"—THE CALL OF
THE YUT (CANDY) BOY RISES CLEAR
AND BECKONING ABOVE THE CLATTER
OF THE MARKET.

GOVERNMENT HOUSE,
SEOUL

If you should visit Seoul, the children there would probably take you to see the three palaces. Two of these palaces are very old, and one is modern. All three wear huge upturned roofs (like the ones on the gate to Seoul) with carved animals and birds peering down from the ends of rafters. The gigantic doors, which are lacquered either red or blue, are almost as bright now as they were when they were painted many hundreds of years ago.

These palaces are very grand with their marble stairways and tall carved columns of cedar wood, their gardens of flowers with cool pools and their great meeting halls. And in the oldest palace is the most impressive sight of all—the Imperial Library.

The children would tell you that these are the memories of their grandfathers; that this is Yesterday's work and that, because of this, these things are honored and loved.

And then they would tell you of their own fathers' work,
Today's work; the digging of new irrigation ditches for
fields of rice and vegetables, the laying of roads to and
from the cities, and the building of railroads, factories,
and clean bright schools. This is their fathers' work, they
would say. It is beautiful for it is useful. It will bring
much happiness to Korea. Because of this, it is loved and
honored also.

The children of Seoul would probably point out too the "Big Bell." This bell is ten feet tall and twenty feet around its bottom edge. It was made in 1468, twenty-four years before Columbus discovered America. As you can see, Korea is indeed a very old country. The Big Bell, like all bells in Korea, has a beautiful, mellow ring. But then, this is not surprising, for Koreans are known throughout the world for their fine bell-making.

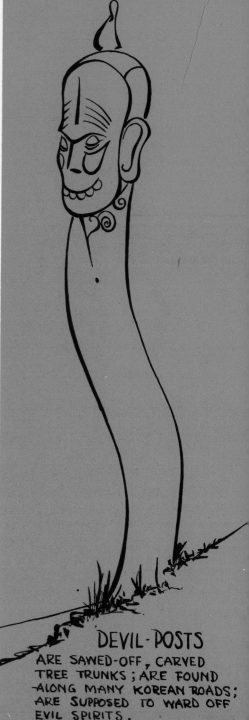

DEVIL·POSTS ARE SAWED-OFF, CARVED TREE TRUNKS; ARE FOUND ALONG MANY KOREAN ROADS; ARE SUPPOSED TO WARD OFF EVIL SPIRITS.

In every Korean town, besides the music of bells, you would hear too the songs of the people. The folk-songs. Koreans love music and make music easily and gladly. You would hear them singing most any time of the day or night; songs of the tiger who lives in their mountains; of wild ducks and geese; of the imperial crane who stalks so haughtily about their rice fields. There are songs which tell the history of Korea, and songs that mothers sing to their babies. Some are songs for dancing, and some are songs for freedom, and some are just for nonsense. There are sad songs and glad songs and play songs and love songs; all kinds of songs. You would hear them everywhere.

JIGGY-CARRIER

JIGGY-CARRIER

A JIGGY IS A WOODEN
FRAME WHICH ENABLES
A MAN TO CARRY AS
MUCH AS 300 POUNDS
ON HIS BACK. JIGGY-
CARRIERS ARE IMPORTANT
MEANS OF TRANSPORTATION.

In Korea, as everywhere else in the world, you would find a friendly people living and working together much as we all live and work together here in America.

In Korea, that country shaped like a finger and stuck, like a finger, straight out into the sea, you would meet your friends, the people: our Korean brothers.

HISTORY

2333 B. C. (?): Tradition places a beginning of Korea here.

57 B. C.: Recorded history begins.

1882 A. D.: Korea and the United States signed a treaty of friendship and trade. Until this year, Korea (the Hermit Kingdom) had had little real contact with the outside world. During the 14th and 15th centuries, however, Korea enjoyed a highly developed civilization, inventing an alphabet and a means of printing books with movable metal type (50 years before Gutenberg), writing histories and encyclopedias, and designing the world's first ironclad ship.

1910: Korea was annexed to Japan. Japanese laws, language, and rulers were imposed on the Korean people.

1919: Korea proclaimed her independence (hoping that the League of Nations would make it come true) and wrote a Provisional Constitution modeled after that of the United States. All of her people were guaranteed freedom of religion, speech, press, and assembly, and her women were given the right to vote. This constitution did not become effective, however, for Japan refused to recognize any such proclamation or constitution, and announced to the world that Koreans were actually Japanese.

1945: Japan was defeated by the Allies during World War II. Korea was free. For the sake of disarming the Japanese soldiers in Korea, it was decided to station United States soldiers in the South and Russian soldiers in the North, dividing north and south at the 38th parallel. This act was tragic for Korea since it prevented the people from getting together to establish their own government to include all of Korea.

1948: The Provisional Government Assembly in South Korea adopted a constitution guaranteeing personal freedom and equality, and establishing a unicameral legislature and state control of foreign trade, transport, and mineral resources. The Assembly chose Syngman Rhee as president, and the Republic of Korea was established on August 15.

1950: War between North and South Korea, with United Nations soldiers supporting the South, the Soviet Union the North.

INDEX

REFERENCES

Asia, Frank G. Carpenter: American Book Co., 1930.

The Epic of Korea, A. Wigfall Green: Public Affairs Press, 1950.

Japan and Korea, Frank G. Carpenter: Doubleday, Page & Co., 1925.

Korea of the Japanese, H. B. Drake: Dodd, Mead & Co., 1930.

Korea Today, George M. McCune: Harvard University Press, 1950.

The Mastery of the Far East, Arthur Judson Brown: Charles Scribner's Sons, 1919.

Modern Korea, Andrew J. Grajdanzev: John Day Co., 1944.

The Pacific: Its Lands & Peoples, Frances Carpenter: American Book Co., 1944.

Tales of a Korean Grandmother, Frances Carpenter: Doubleday & Company, Inc., 1947.

The Truth About Korea, Carlton Waldo Kendall (Containing the Document of Provisional Constitution): Korean National Association, 1919.

The New International Year Book: Funk & Wagnalls Co.
  1947: "Korea," Joseph P. Blank.
      "Korean Literature, Arts & Crafts," Evelyn B. McCune.
  1948: "Korea," George M. McCune.
      "Korean Literature, Arts & Crafts," Evelyn B. McCune.
  1949: "Korea," Carl F. Bartz, Jr.
      "Korean Literature, Arts & Crafts," Evelyn B. McCune.
  1950: "Korea," Carl F. Bartz, Jr.
  1951: "Korea," Carl F. Bartz, Jr.
  1952: "Korea," Arthur L. Grey, Jr.
10 Eventful Years (1937-1946), Vol. II, Walter Yust, Editor: Encyclopedia Britannica.
      "Korea," pp. 805-807.
"A History of Democratic Movement in Korea," by Yu Chin O. *Korea, The Monthly Magazine*, April, 1951: Korean Pacific Press, Washington, D.C.